DSLR Photography for Beginners

A Beginners Guide to Mastering the Basics of Digital Photography

Giovanni Moranti

Copyright ©2017 by Giovanni Moranti
All rights reserved. No part of this book may be reproduced or transmitted in any form or by any means without written permission from the author.

Table of Contents

Table of Contents 2
From the author 3
Introduction 4
Chapter One: Aperture 5
Chapter Two: Shutter Speed 8
Chapter Three: ISO 10
Chapter Four: Specialized Lenses 12
    Focal length 12
    Telephoto lens 13
    Wide angle lens 14
    Zoom lens 15
    Macro lens 15
    Fisheye lens 15
Chapter Five: Filters 17
Chapter Six: Lighting, Framing, & Focus 19
    Lighting 19
    Framing 21
    Focus 22
Before you go 24

From the author

Hi I would like to start of by saying thank you for downloading this book and I hope it gives you the beginner photographer a great understanding of the basics to do with the DSLR camera and instant improvement in the quality of your shots.

If you enjoy this book I would like to ask you a favor, would you be so kind as to leave a review on Amazon for me as it will help other people interested in taking up photography decide if it is the right book for them.

Thank you,

Giovanni

Introduction

Digital photography is the standard for today. The camera sold today are digital. But why is digital photography now the leader? All photography is an attempt to capture an image by focusing light through a lens and recording that image. Analog photography, the precursor to digital photography, used film containing light-sensitive chemicals which would darken or change in color when they were hit by light. The film had to be processed which was time-consuming and prone to human error along the way. More importantly it was expensive for material and labor. Digital photography entered the scene which allowed for photographs to be developed and preserved in a much faster and less expensive fashion.

With digital photography the light from the land is focused on to an electronic light sensor which is hooked up to a computer processing chip so that the image is created digitally and stored inside of digital memory. You can see that image immediately on the screen of your camera, you can transmit that image from one device to another, edit it on your computer, and publishes online almost instantaneously. No longer do you have to wait hours or days before you see how the pictures turned out. You can literally check the image as soon as you take it. You can take as many shots as you want without having to purchase more film. More importantly you can save all of your images without having to get each one printed. Making copies is simple and you don't lose fidelity along the way.

Essentially digital photography has taken the guesswork out of picture taking.
So now you know that the D stands for "digital". But what

about the rest to Mark the S LR stands for "single lens reflex". This simply refers to the type of viewfinder on your camera. The viewfinder is placed either above or beside your camera lens and it focuses separately from your camera lens. The image that you see through your viewfinder is not precisely what will appear in the photo but it can be very close. This type of camera is beneficial in photography because it lets you change the lenses.

You can use a telephoto lens, a close-up lens, or other lenses with different aperture settings to get the picture that you want most. These cameras are always equipped with removable lenses so you can replace the lens at any time with something more suited to your preference. Sensors are built into the viewing display so you can tell whether you have enough light at your current aperture setting and your current shutter speed. You can see how well focused your image is.

Chapter One: Aperture

The aperture refers to how wide your shutter opening is when you take a picture. If you have a wide aperture, you will have a wider opening which means more light comes into your pictures. This is best suited for situations where you don't have a lot of natural light. When you are trying to take pictures at night for example, a wider aperture lets you capture more of the limited and available lighting. But the downside is a wider aperture also creates a shallower depth of focus there are parts of your picture which might not be in focus. For some people this can be a good thing because it provides the effect they are looking for but it might not work for everybody.

The aperture of your camera is measured in what is called "f stop" you might also see it listed as the "f number". This is a technical meaning. It involves a two-based logarithmic scale. This means that one f number difference will double or half the amount of light that comes in the camera. The mathematical formula used to calculate this is not important especially as a beginner. What you need to know is that the lower the number, the larger the aperture. So having a setting of F1 is a very wide aperture but having a setting of F8 is very narrow. Your lens will come with a range of apertures controlled by a device called the diaphragm. The diaphragm works similarly to the way the Iris in your eye functions. This is not a feature of the changeable part of your lens. It is part of your camera mechanism located behind the lens. Each lens you purchase is sold with a description or a rating which specifies your minimum and maximum aperture amounts. They refer to this as the lens speed. The reason it is called speed is because it affects how fast your shutter speed has to be with that lens.

Your shutter speed and your aperture are inversely related. If you have a wide aperture you need to have a faster shutter speed for any light conditions. Again, the wide aperture left in more light but the faster shutter speed let in less because it produces the time that your sensors are exposed to light.

You have to take into consideration how your picture will be framed when you are looking at it through the viewer. If you have a narrow aperture it might be appropriate for taking pictures when you are standing outside in the bright sun. SLR cameras come with what is called an automatic aperture control. This will set your aperture to the widest setting possible for your lens and appropriately metered the light. It will close the aperture down to a level that is appropriate as soon as you take your picture.

Digital SLR cameras can be set up so they adjust the shutter speed and aperture automatically. There is a semi-automatic adjustment referred to as "aperture priority". When you use this, you will manually choose the aperture you want and let the camera automatically choose your shutter speed and ISO sensitivity so that you get the best exposure. This technique lets you control the type of focus you want without manually setting all three of these variables.

So which affect is better? Narrow aperture and slow shutter speed or wide aperture and fast shutter speed? This depends entirely on what you're trying to capture in your picture. If you want to take a photo where your immediate center of focus is a single subject, perhaps photographing an animal or person, you can get the narrow aperture and slow shutter speed so that the background is blurry but your subject remains in focus. Conversely if you want to get a panoramic shot which provides your friends and family with a clear view of the city landscape you saw outside of your hotel window, the office it would be better suited so that they can get all of the detail possible. If you use aperture priority you can take pictures without having to select everything yourself each time. But, if you play around with the three different settings, you might end up taking a picture with an effect that you didn't plan on but in the end truly enjoy.

Chapter Two: Shutter Speed

We've already talked about the inverse relationship between shutter speed and aperture. Remember that a fast shutter speed will not let in as much light as a slower shutter speed. So if you want a narrow aperture, so that you can get a high depth of field image, you need to have a slower shutter speed. Your shutter speed is also referred to as exposure time. This is measured in terms of the amount of time that your camera shutter remains open while taking your pictures. A fast shutter speed means a shorter exposure time, and a slower shutter speed means a longer exposure time. For example, if you are trying to take a nighttime photo of the city lights, you need your shutter time to be much slower so that you have a longer exposure time. Having a longer exposure time means the shutter will stay open and capture more light. This is how you are able to capture city lights at night. If you tried to take the same picture with a short exposure time you wouldn't be able to capture as much light and the image would likely come out very black.

You can use kind exposure where the shutter will remain open for several seconds so that you can photograph something where there is poor lighting. When you do this, just like photographing a nighttime picture of the city lights, you need to have a tripod so that you stabilize the camera. You might think that your hand is steady, but if you are holding the camera for 30 seconds or longer any single movement of your hand will cause the image come out blurry. The image has to remain precisely stable for the full amount of time that the shutter is open.

A slower shutter speed will create a greater effect from the camera motion which is why you want that tripod. Of course what matters most here is the relative motion of your camera and the subject. If you want to take a picture of a moving object using a slow shutter speed, it can create a blurred image of that object which is usually how people get images of car lights along the highway as blurred streams of light with the lights of the city buildings crystal-clear. Using a fast shutter speed will make the objects appear crisp with less blurring and better definition. Neither option is better than the other. It is all simply based on what effect you want to create your picture.

Your shutter speed is measured in a fraction of a second. The standard shutter speed is 1\1000 of a second all the way up to one full second. Your shutter, just like the diaphragm, is part of your camera body and not part of the lens. In order for you to properly expose your photo you need to have a slow shutter speed or a narrow aperture and vice versa. What you decide is contingent upon the specific lighting settings and conditions that you have.

Chapter Three: ISO

The third factor you have to consider to determine the exposure of your picture is called your light sensitivity referred to as ISO sensitivity. This term is taken from an international standard measurement for the film. The measurement doesn't actually apply directly to digital photography but it was borrowed and today is displayed as 200, 400, and so on. The higher your sensitivity, the less light is required to produce a particular exposure. With more light sensitivity your camera will give you picture quality with a narrow aperture and faster shutter speed. If you are trying to take pictures in a dimly lit room or you don't want to create a blurred motion affect, you can use this third factor to get the picture you desire. Originally this measurement referred to the type of film speed you had.

Today, digital photography sometimes it suffers from very high light sensitivity which is referred to as "noise". This is something that you don't see with your actual eye but chances are you have taken and printed a photo once before which looked perfectly fine in your camera viewfinder but then was grainy in the texture when you tried to print it. This is called noise. In almost no situation do you actually want expect grainy quality.
It is for this reason that there is often a trade-off between your shutter speed and aperture compared to the light sensitivity. It is best for you to set your ISO sensitivity to as low a level as possible given your conditions. If your picture can be taken at a lower sensitivity with a narrow aperture and fast shutter speed, do it. Some photos might benefit from higher light sensitivity. Photos that normally require flash can be taken without flash if you use a higher ISO sensitivity. Doing so will avoid the distorting impact that a flash can have. Some photos

taken in dim light settings also benefit from a high ISO sensitivity rather than a wider aperture with a slower shutter speed. Again, there is no right or wrong. The settings you choose are really all based on what it is you want in your final picture.

You can play around, thankfully, with a digital camera and take multiple pictures of the same image or setting using different aperture, shutter speed, and ISO settings. One of the best ways to learn what things you enjoy giving different situations is to practice taking pictures of a few different items at common times during the day. You might, for example, spend five minutes taking a picture of your local park in the morning, then during the daylight, then at sunset, and finally at night. When you practice, use all of the different settings and combinations of the three features, marking in a notebook which settings you used for which image. Then you can go back and look at the image and figure out which settings you prefer in order to capture certain things, focus on different elements in your picture, or get the best lighting. Regularly practicing like this can help you figure out what your personal preferences so that later when you go back and try to achieve the same type of focus for lighting in a different setting, you know which shutter speed, aperture, and ISO want.

These three elements work together to render a photo that captures different elements to a different degree. Right now the most important thing for you to understand is how these three things interact with one another and change the exposure of your photo.

Chapter Four: Specialized Lenses

The biggest advantage to using a DSLR camera is that you can change your lens. When you buy a digital camera it will come with a single lens usually moderate zoom capabilities. This lens might be good for your regular camera taking when you start to familiarize yourself with functionality. However, as you get better and more confident with your camera, you can detach this lens and replace it. There are many types of specialized lenses out there. The most common ones that you will use as a photographer include a zoom lens, macro lens which is also referred to as the close-up lens, a wide angle lens, a telephoto lens, and a fisheye lens.

Before you purchase your lens, understand that it is a significant investment so you want to do research before you go out and start a collection. Figure out based on your camera's manual, which lenses are fully compatible. The mountings are fairly standard especially if you buy a lens from the same brand as your camera, but some of them might not physically mount to your camera. You also want to make sure that you choose a lens based on the type of photography you want to do. A fast lens offers many advantages for indoor photography for portraits. A slower lens might be less expensive and ideally suited for outdoor photography especially if you want a broad depth of field. The biggest thing you want to consider is what type of photography you want to practice.

Focal length

One of the variables between different lenses is the focal length. This is actually one of the main ways that lenses are categorized. A zoom lens, a normal lens, a telephoto lens, and a wide angle lens are divided because of the focal length they provide. Your eyes also have a focal length which is the distance from the center plane of your eye to your retina. The standard focal length for your high is 22 mm. But of course your camera has a larger light sensor than your eyeball so it has a larger focal length. For most cameras the standard focal length is between 35 mm and 85 mm.

Why does this matter? Well, first, the focal length varies the magnification that you get. The longer the focal length, the bigger your magnification. The shorter your focal length the smaller things will appear in your image then they did to the naked eye. Focal length also increases or reduces the depth of field. As a rule, the shorter your focal length, the greater your depth of field. Lenses can be one fixed focal length, if they are a prime lens, or they can be made to adjust. If your lens adjusts it is called a zoom lens because it has a variable focal length. There are many types of zoom lenses and obviously be larger the city capabilities, the more expensive the lens is going to be. When you are purchasing your lenses there has to be a trade-off between picture quality and convenience. A super zoom lens might maximize how far you can take a picture but it might not work as well in terms of quality. You might not get the same high quality photos that you could with a standard lens.

Telephoto lens

The telephoto lens is one which magnifies your image. These

are rated based on their magnification. You might have one that is rated 5X which means it magnifies five times the normal size. The reason you would want a telephoto lens is to shoot subjects that is really far away usually because you can't get close enough to take a good photo or the subject just doesn't want you to. A lot of wildlife photography and sports photography uses a telephoto lens. You are much safer taking pictures of polar bears from your boat than you are trying to get on the ice with them another reason that people use a telephoto lens is to create a very narrow depth of field in portrait photography. So if you want a crisply defined portrait with the entire background out of focus, then the telephoto lens might be best for you. Of course as a beginner you should hold off on this costly investment until you have need to use it.

Wide angle lens

A wide angle lens does the exact opposite of the telephoto lens. It usually has a short focal length of 35 mm or less which captures a wider view. The magnification of the wide angle lens is usually negative, meaning it makes objects appear smaller in the photo than they were in reality. A lot of tourists enjoy having a wide angle lens as their first lens purchase because it is perfect for taking pictures of buildings, architecture, and panoramic shots. It is one of the most commonly used extra lenses when you go on vacation and want to take pictures of the city landscape for larger groups of people.

Zoom lens

A zoom lens is essentially an adjustable wide angle or telephoto lens. The difference between the prime lens and zoom lens is that it has a variable focal length. You can adjust it in one or both directions which makes it convenient when you are taking different types of pictures. You do not have to carry around multiple lenses when you go on vacation if you have a simple zoom lens.

Macro lens

The macro lens is the close-up lens which gives you much closer focus for smaller objects. People who want to photograph things like flowers or insects will typically use the macro lens. The lens itself doesn't have to be extremely close to the subject in order for you to take the photo which is what allows people to take pictures of things like bugs without scaring them away. Macro lenses are perfect for nature photography but as well as portraiture. You get high quality and meets a shallow depth of field. The difference between the macro lens and the telephoto lenses that the macro lens provides a very tight and sharply focused image on a single object with every detail showing up crisply.

Fisheye lens

The fisheye lens is an extremely wide angle lens which adds a type of spatial distortion to your picture. The central part of your picture will look enlarged in the peripheral portions will look smaller with clarity reducing as you get further away from the center. The angle provided by this type of lens is usually 180° but you can take up to 220°. You get a very circular shape with this particular lens which creates a circular image inside of the frame which is distorted with most of the picture being flat. A lot of people use the fisheye lens for things like landscape photography.

Chapter Five: Filters

Filters are transparent attachments that altered the light. You put them on your camera lens to get different effects. There are many filters today which can help you create some of the same adjustments that you could theoretically produce in Photoshop, but obviously without having to use Photoshop. With a round filter you can simply mount it to your camera lens.

A polarizing filter is one of the first filters you will probably buy as a beginner. It removes reflections and is perfect for outdoor photography under natural light conditions. It will enhance color so the water looks more transparent. This is achieved by removing the reflections from the surface of the water. A polarizing filter will also remove the glare from the sunlight or from the right surfaces. Depending on how it is positioned your polarizing filter lets you achieve different effects. Again, if you like to shoot pictures through or around bodies of water this filter is very useful because it will remove the glare of from the sunlight reflected off the water. It also works well to change the appearance and color of the sky. The colors will appear much brighter. Obviously this is not necessarily a good or bad thing but simply based on what picture quality you want to achieve. Understand that with this type of filter it will dim the amount of light going into your lens so you probably need to have a wider aperture and slower shutter speed than you normally use.

Neutral density filter is another option for cutting down the amount of light going into your lens. It reduces the intensity of the light so that you still get the same color balance you see with your eyes but at a reduced volume. Photographers can use this filter for things like shooting a picture of a waterfall at a slower shutter speed so you get that motion suggestive, blurred impact. Close-up pictures of flowers with the entire garden background blurred is another option for the neutral density filter. You can even take pictures of a boat out on the lake with all of the clouds in the sky blurred and the boat zoomed in with crystal clarity.

The ultraviolet filter will block ultraviolet light this is a natural part of sunlight, precisely the part of the sun which causes sunburns and tans. You can't see it with your eyes but your camera will typically pick it up. By blocking it out you can restore the image to precisely what you saw with your eyes.

Chapter Six: Lighting, Framing, & Focus

Now that you understand the basics of how your camera works it is important to understand how to best compose your picture. Composition simply refers to how you change what is in your picture and what effect is created. You can change the composure of your photo by simply changing what is in it. If you are taking pictures of a monument, you could take a picture of the monument itself, cutting out the other tourists or you could try changing the setup so that the focus of your picture is a father helping his daughter tie her shoe directly in front of the monument, with the monument in the background. If you are taking pictures of people you can alter things like poses, the makeup, the hairstyles or clothing, even the background. Wedding pictures, for example, typically consist of the same few poses but simply scattered across the wedding location.

Beyond the simple alteration the three things you can do to change the composition of your picture include the lighting, the framing, and the focus.

Lighting

If you are in a studio, you can control the lighting just as well as the subject matter. Of course if you are outside, it isn't as easy. However, when outside, one of the things you can do to change the lighting is to change the time of day or the weather conditions under which photos are taken. You can get a dimmer light on an overcast day compared to a sunshiny day.

Different lighting conditions appear at night or under moonlight and they would in the day. Another way to control lighting outside is to start from the other end. Adjust your aperture, ISO sensitivity and shutter speed to increase or reduce the amount of light that enters your camera. You can deliberately take an overexposed or underexposed photo. If you want to give a washed out appearance than overexposing the photo is best. You can bring up detailing things that are in the shadows with this technique. Under exposing can deepen the colors in certain parts of your picture and make other parts less visible.

As you continue to take pictures you'll get a better feel for what things your camera can achieve. But no matter which camera you have, abide by these three rules:

1. A wide aperture will let in more light but it will reduce your depth of field.
2. A slow shutter speed will let in more light but will increase the blurring of the subject.
3. High capital ISO sensitivity will increase the brightness of your picture but also increase the graininess.

Keeping these rules in mind you can adjust your sensitivity to produce the effect you want for your photo. Other rules include the following:

- The broader your source of light, the softer your life will be. A narrow light will provide you with a sharper light. If you want lower textures or softer shadows in contrast, a broad light is best.
- A broad light allows light to hit your subject from many different directions. With portrait photography a soft effect can be achieved by putting your subject right next to the window without direct sunlight.

- The more distant the source of light, the harder the light will be. Additionally, the more distant your source of life, the more it begins.
- The closer your light source is to the subject of your photo, the sharper it will be on objects farther away. Lighting from the front will soften the texture.
- Lighting from above, below, or the side will sharpen the texture.
- Shadows will generate a bigger sense of volume. Back lighting will create highly diffuse lighting but it also makes it difficult for light metering.
- Finally, even the light your eyes see as white actually contains some color

Framing

The way you frame your photo refers to what things you include and deliberately exclude from your picture. Obviously in the studio you have a bit more control over what things actually go into your picture compared to taking photos outside. Even outside you want to figure out what should be in the center of your photo. Figure out what you want at the edge of your photo. Sometimes you can set up natural objects to frame your picture. If you're taking a picture outside, the wall of a local bakery can serve as the frame around a picture of a monument, person, or anything else. You can use things like a tree limb to create a border around the nature photo you take.

Decide how much you want in your picture. Control this by changing the position you are actually using when you take your shot, as well as how zoomed in or out your picture is. Choose the angle carefully as well so that everything is the right size in position to the other elements within the photo. Your image should draw the eye immediately to what you want to be the center of your attention. The center of the photo or image does not literally have to be the middle of the picture. Use the rule of thirds to align your subject's slightly off center but frame it so that the eye is still drawn to the subject in question. To do this you simply divide the image you see in your camera into nine parts of equal size with two horizontal lines into vertical lines. The four intersections of these lines are the main points of interest in your picture, the areas where your eyes are drawn naturally. Your photo should be composed so that the subject matter hits one of these points and the people looking at your picture are naturally drawn to it.

Focus

The final way to frame your picture is the focus. Consider what the center of focus is for your picture, how sharply you want that focus to be, and how sharply the focus will be in the rest of your photographs. In almost every case the center of the picture should be in sharp focus but there are a few exceptions. Once you control the focus of your main subject, you want to control the depth of field with the aperture and then control the blurring effects with your shutter speed.

All of this is again in no way right or wrong. This is what makes photography and art form. You can read through all of these tips time and time again but there are any number of possibilities for every type of photo you plan to take. It is up to you to use your artistic capabilities and your camera to figure out the settings that best capture the image you want. You might want to have speed or movement conveyed in your picture with a blurred effect. You might want to capture every bit of detail in a collector plate at a museum. You might want the subject of your picture to be sharp and clear with everything around it blurred. You might want everything in your picture to be focused clearly and crisply. This is all up to you to decide. Your camera is the perfect tool for testing multiple images and capturing photos exactly the way you want.

Before you go

If you enjoyed this book, please consider signing up for my mailing list - http://eepurl.com/dknzaD

Finally I would like to thank you again for downloading this book and hope you have got something out of it.

Before you go I would like to ask a favor, if you enjoyed this book would you be kind enough to click on the link below and leave a review to help make this book more accessible to other readers.

Yes I would like to leave a review:
https://www.amazon.com/review/create-review?ie=UTF8&asin=B077WHTDPF&ref_=dpx_acr_wr_link&#

Thank you

www.ingramcontent.com/pod-product-compliance
Lightning Source LLC
Chambersburg PA
CBHW071002220526
45471CB00007B/3137